Carrying the Glory of God: Igniting the End Time Revival

Bill Vincent

Published by RWG Publishing, 2022.

While every precaution has been taken in the preparation of this book, the publisher assumes no responsibility for errors or omissions, or for damages resulting from the use of the information contained herein.

CARRYING THE GLORY OF GOD: IGNITING THE END TIME REVIVAL

First edition. August 31, 2022.

Copyright © 2022 Bill Vincent.

Written by Bill Vincent.

Also by Bill Vincent

Building a Prototype Church: Divine Strategies Released
Experience God's Love: By Revival Waves of Glory School of the Supernatural
Glory: Expanding God's Presence
Glory: Increasing God's Presence
Glory: Kingdom Presence of God
Glory: Pursuing God's Presence
Glory: Revival Presence of God
Rapture Revelations: Jesus Is Coming
The Prototype Church: Heaven's Strategies for Today's Church
The Secret Place of God's Power
Transitioning Into a Prototype Church: New Church Arising
Spiritual Warfare Made Simple
Aligning With God's Promises
A Closer Relationship With God
Armed for Battle: Spiritual Warfare Battle Commands
Breakthrough of Spiritual Strongholds
Desperate for God's Presence: Understanding Supernatural Atmospheres
Destroying the Jezebel Spirit: How to Overcome the Spirit Before It Destroys You!
Discerning Your Call of God

Glory: Expanding God's Presence: Discover How to Manifest God's Glory

Glory: Kingdom Presence Of God: Secrets to Becoming Ambassadors of Christ

Satan's Open Doors: Access Denied

Spiritual Warfare: The Complete Collection

The War for Spiritual Battles: Identify Satan's Strategies

Understanding Heaven's Court System: Explosive Life Changing Secrets

A Godly Shaking: Don't Create Waves

Faith: A Connection of God's Power

Global Warning: Prophetic Details Revealed

Overcoming Obstacles

Spiritual Leadership: Kingdom Foundation Principles

Glory: Revival Presence of God: Discover How to Release Revival Glory

Increasing Your Prophetic Gift: Developing a Pure Prophetic Flow

Millions of Churches: Why Is the World Going to Hell?

The Supernatural Realm: Discover Heaven's Secrets

The Unsearchable Riches of Christ: Chosen to be Sons of God

Deep Hunger: God Will Change Your Appetite Toward Him

Defeating the Demonic Realm

Glory: Increasing God's Presence: Discover New Waves of God's Glory

Growing In the Prophetic: Developing a Prophetic Voice

Healing After Divorce: Grace, Mercy and Remarriage

Love is Waiting

Awakening of Miracles: Personal Testimonies of God's Healing Power

Deception and Consequences Revealed: You Shall Know the Truth and the Truth Shall Set You Free

Overcoming the Power of Lust

Are You a Follower of Christ: Discover True Salvation

Cover Up and Save Yourself: Revealing Sexy is Not Sexy

Heaven's Court System: Bringing Justice for All

The Angry Fighter's Story: Harness the Fire Within

The Wrestler: The Pursuit of a Dream

Beginning the Courts of Heaven: Understanding the Basics

Breaking Curses: Legal Rights in the Courts of Heaven

Writing and Publishing a Book: Secrets of a Christian Author

How to Write a Book: Step by Step Guide

The Anointing: Fresh Oil of God's Presence

Spiritual Leadership: Kingdom Foundation Principles Second Edition

The Courts of Heaven: How to Present Your Case

The Jezebel Spirit: Tactics of Jezebel's Control

Heaven's Angels: The Nature and Ranking of Angels

Don't Know What to Do?: Discover Promotion in the Wilderness

Word of the Lord: Prophetic Word for 2020

The Coronavirus Prophecy

Increase Your Anointing: Discover the Supernatural

Apostolic Breakthrough: Birthing God's Purposes

The Healing Power of God: Releasing the Power of the Holy Spirit

The Secret Place of God's Power: Revelations of God's Word

The Rapture: Details of the Second Coming of Christ

Increase of Revelation and Restoration: Reveal, Recover & Restore

Restoration of the Soul: The Presence of God Changes Everything

Building a Prototype Church: The Church is in a Season of Profound of Change

Keys to Receiving Your Miracle: Miracles Happen Today

The Resurrection Power of God: Great Exploits of God

Transitioning to the Prototype Church: The Church is in a Season of Profound of Transition

Waves of Revival: Expect the Unexpected

The Stronghold of Jezebel: A True Story of a Man's Journey

Glory: Pursuing God's Presence: Revealing Secrets

Like a Mighty Rushing Wind

Steps to Revival

Supernatural Power

The Goodness of God

The Secret to Spiritual Strength

The Glorious Church's Birth: Understanding God's Plan For Our Lives

God's Presence Has a Profound Impact On Us

Spiritual Battles of the Mind: When All Hell Breaks Loose, Heaven Sends Help

A Godly Shaking Coming to the Church: Churches are Being Rerouted

Relationship with God in a New Way

The Spirit of God's Anointing: Using the Holy Spirit's Power in You

The Magnificent Church: God's Power Is Being Manifested

Miracles Are Awakened: Today is a Day of Miracles

Prepared to Fight: The Battle of Deliverance

The Journey of a Faithful: Adhering to the teachings of Jesus Christ

Ascension to the Top of Spiritual Mountains: Putting an End to Pain Cycles

After Divorce Recovery: When I Think of Grace, I Think of Mercy and Remarriage

A Greater Sense of God's Presence: Learn How to Make God's Glory Visible

Do Not Allow the Enemy to Steal: To a Crown of Righteousness, a Crown of Thorns

There Are Countless Churches: What is the Cause of Global Doom?

Creating a Model Church: The Church is Undergoing Considerable Upheaval

Developing Your Prophetic Ability: Creating a Flow of Pure Prophetic Intent

Christ's Limitless Riches Are Unsearchable: God Has Chosen Us to Be His Sons

Faith is a Link Between God's Might and Ours

Increasing the Presence of God: The Revival of the End-Times Is Approaching

Getting a Prophecy for Yourself: Unlocking Your Prophecies with Prophetic Keys

Getting Rid of the Jezebel Spirit: Before the Spirit Destroys You, Here's How to Overcome It!

Getting to Know Heaven's Court System: Secrets That Will Change Your Life

God's Resurrected Presence: Revival Glory is Being Released

God's Presence In His Kingdom: Secrets to Becoming Christ's Ambassadors

God's Healing Ability: The Holy Spirit's Power is Being Released

God's Power of Resurrection: God's Great Exploits

- Heaven's Supreme Court: Providing Equal Justice for All
- Increasing God's Presence in Our Lives: God's Glory Has Reached New Heights
- Jezebel's Stronghold: This is the Story of an Actual Man's Journey
- Making the Shift to the Model Church: The Church Is In the Midst of a Major Shift
- Overcoming Lust's Influence: The Way to Victory
- Pursuing God's Presence: Disclosing Information
- The Plan to Take Over America: Restoring, We the People and the Power of God
- Revelation and Restoration Are Increasing: The Process That Reveals, Recovers, and Restores
- Burn In the Presence of the Lord
- Revival Tidal Waves: Be Prepared for the Unexpected
- Taking down the Demonic Realm: Curses and Revelations of Demonic Spirits
- The Apocalypse: Details about Christ's Second Coming
- The Hidden Resource of God's Power
- The Open Doors of Satan: Access is Restricted
- The Secrets to Getting Your Miracle
- The Truth About Deception and Its Consequences
- The Universal World: Discover the Mysteries of Heaven
- Warning to the World: Details of Prophecies Have Been Revealed
- Wonders and Significance: God's Glory in New Waves
- Word of the Lord
- Why Is There No Lasting Revival: It's Time For the Next Move of God
- A Double New Beginning: A Prophetic Word, the Best Is Yet to Come

Your Most Productive Season Ever: The Anointing to Get Things Done

Break Free From Prison: No More Bondage for the Saints

Breaking Strongholds: Taking Steps to Freedom

Carrying the Glory of God: Igniting the End Time Revival

Breakthrough Over the Enemies Attack on Resources: An Angel Called Breakthrough

Days of Breakthrough: Your Time is Now

Empowered For the Unprecedented: Extraordinary Days Ahead

The Ultimate Guide to Self-Publishing: How to Write, Publish, and Promote Your Book for Free

The Art of Writing: A Comprehensive Guide to Crafting Your Masterpiece

The Non-Fiction Writer's Guide: Mastering Engaging Narratives

Spiritual Leadership (Large Print Edition): Kingdom Foundation Principles

Desperate for God's Presence (Large Print Edition): Understanding Supernatural Atmospheres

From Writer to Marketer: How to Successfully Promote Your Self-Published Book

Unleashing Your Inner Author: A Step-by-Step Guide to Crafting Your Own Bestseller

Becoming a YouTube Sensation: A Guide to Success

Watch for more at https://revivalwavesofgloryministries.com/.

Carrying the Glory of God Igniting the End Time Revival

SUMMARY KEYWORDS
God, revival, fire, burning, Holy Spirit, Jesus, spirit, shake, glory, prayed, ignited, nation, father, atmosphere, multitudes, presence, shadow, wonders miracles, wonders, predestined, transformed, unveiled face

The flame of God

Leviticus 6:12, 13 And the fire upon the altar shall be burning in it; it shall not be put out: and the priest shall burn wood on it every morning, and lay the burnt offering in order upon it; and he shall burn thereon the fat of the peace offerings. The fire shall ever be burning upon the altar; it shall never go out.

Over 100 years ago, the power of the Holy Spirit descended upon the nation of Wales, ushering in over 100,000 souls into the Kingdom of God and 10s of millions throughout the world. This revival fire was ignited in the heart of a young man named Evan Roberts.

Evan Roberts had been earnestly praying for revival for 10 years. And he came to a point where he was troubled in his spirit over the condition of the church. And after seeking the baptism and fullness of the Holy Spirit, Evan was taken into a season of visitation. He would be awakened by the Lord at 1 am each night and he would be caught up in divine communion with God for four hours.

At times, the light and glory of God would rest so powerfully upon him that his bed would physically shake, Roberts was quoted as saying, I have reached out my hand and touched the flame I am burning and waiting for a sign Evan Roberts prayed and a spark was released, igniting a world-changing national move of God.

A month before the revival broke out, Evan was attending an evangelistic meeting. For years, The Evangelist had prayed that God would raise a simple boy from the mines or the fields, not from the universities, so that pride and intellectualism wouldn't be fed, but rather all the glory would go to God and God had found his man in Evan Roberts. On October 31, 1904, Everett invited a group of young people to come and gather as he shared his heart for revival with the 16 young people, the fire of God fell upon them. And within two weeks the entire nation was set ablaze with revival fire. The heartfelt prayer of this revival became to send the Spirit now for Jesus' sake.

The Holy Spirit heard that prayer. And suddenly men and women began to give their lives to Jesus and repent of their sins. Soon a transformation of the entire society began to take place. Prostitutes were getting saved and opening Bible studies. Bars and movie houses were closing. So many of the coal miners were coming to Jesus that they had to retrain their mules because they were unaccustomed to commands without curse words. The mines became a common place for prayer meetings, even Bibles were selling out in the local bookstores. It is said that God's presence so permeated the nation of Wales. That as you stepped foot onto Welsh soil, you would be overcome with the manifested glory and presence of the Holy Spirit's 1000s were struck to the heart and were unable to escape the convicting power of the Holy Spirit. Men and women openly confess their sins and gave their lives completely to God. It was an awakening that shook the world. Father God, we cry out for awakening to shake our nation once again. Father God as Evan Roberts reached out his hand and touch the flame of God. So, Father God, we reach out our hands right now to you. And we touch the living flame of God let the spirit of awakening be ignited today.

Carrying the Glory

And believers were increasingly added to the Lord, multitudes of both men and women, so that they brought the sick out into the streets and laid them on beds and couches, that at least the shadow of Peter passing by, might fall on some of them. Also, a multitude gathered from the surrounding cities to Jerusalem, bringing sick people and those who are tormented by unclean spirits. And they were all huge.

2 Kings 13:21 So it was, as they were burying a man, that suddenly they spied a band of raiders, and they put the man in the tomb of Elisha. And when the man was let down and touched the bones of Elisha, he revived and stood on his feet.

Father God, we want to carry your glory in our lives. Father God, we want to be so full of your glory, that the very atmosphere of heaven would become the atmosphere in which we live.

Fill us with Your glory today. Fill us so much with your glory that we would carry your presence on the Earth. Father God, I pray today, to make a church without walls. Break down the walls that can find your glory within a good church service.

Father God, let us be so full of your glory, so full of Your Spirit, that the atmosphere of the Holy Spirit would become the atmosphere that fills our lives.

I pray that wherever we would go, we would learn how to carry Your presence with us in our homes, in our workplaces, in our schools, and our neighborhoods that we would carry the very manifested presence of the Holy Spirit. As Peter would come into a city The Bible says that they would bring out the sick and those that were oppressed out into the streets. Multitudes would gather and as Peter would walk down the street sick father, we want to carry so much of your glory that our shadows you're sick. Father God, we want to carry so much of your glory. That is everywhere we go. We would see the demonstration power of Your Spirit. Father God, signs, and wonders would follow us everywhere we go. Signs and wonders in the streets. Signs and wonders in our neighborhoods. Signs and wonders in the marketplace. Make our shadows dangerous make my shadow dangerous May I be so full of the Spirit? Let the atmosphere of my life be the atmosphere of Your glory let my home be full of Your glory, let my life be full of Your glory. And when people see me, they see Your glory. That when people come into my presence they come into the presence of God. Let us be so full of the glory of God that the spirit of revival would be released through our lives.

And when the man was let down and touched the bones of Elisha, he revived and stood on his feet. Father God let us be so full of Your glory, that even our bones would be anointed. Let us be so full of the glory of God that the spirit of revival would be released through our lives. Father God, let the atmosphere around us become saturated with the presence of the Holy Spirit, shepherd us, Lord, as carriers of Your glory. Release Your glory from the upper room to the streets. Release that apostolic anointing signs, wonders, and miracles everywhere we go, send us Lord as carriers of Your glory.

Beholding Your glory

Isaiah 60:1 Arise, shine for your light is come, and the glory of the Lord has risen upon you. For behold, the darkness shall cover the earth, and deep darkness the people, but the Lord will arise over you, and His glory will be seen upon you.

2 Corinthians 3:17, 18 Now the Lord is the Spirit and where the Spirit of the Lord is, there is liberty. But we all with unveiled face, beholding as in a mirror, the glory of the Lord, are being transformed into the same image, from glory to glory, just as by the Spirit of

Romans 8:29, 30 For whom He foreknew, He also predestined to be conformed to the image of His Son, that He might be the firstborn among many brethren. Moreover, who He predestined, these He also called, who we called, these He also justified and who he justified, these He also glorified.

Father God, as David prayed in the Psalms, one thing I have desired of the Lord, that will I seek, that I may dwell in the house of the Lord all the days of my life, to behold the beauty of the Lord, and to inquire in His temple. Father today my heart cries out to my spirit man, roles within me, that I might behold the beauty of the Lord. Father God, I come today, to behold the Lord in this place, in this place of your glory, I behold your face I behold Your glory Father, I thank you that even as the darkness increases over the face of the earth, so the light of Your glory increases in me.

Father God, I pray today that your glory would arise over me. Father God, I pray that Your light would shine upon me. Father God, I pray that I would behold You in the fullness of who you are. Behold Your glory I see Your light radiating upon me. Your glory fills me now. Your very countenance shines upon me for where the Spirit of the Lord is, there is liberty. There is liberty. Liberty, I behold you, as in a mirror, as in the mirror, I behold the glory of the Lord. So, I am transformed into that same image. Even now because I behold your glory. Lord, You transform me. Father God, you change me into Your image. For I've been destined, I have been destined to be conformed to the image of Christ, even before I was born, God, you predestined me to be conformed to the very image and nature of Your son transformed me. Let the glory of God fill my deepest place. Lord, even as I Look upon your face, even as I behold you now transform my inner man with just one look, I am changed forever. Just one touch of Your glory and I will never be the same again. Just one touch. I have to say just one mark. Father God have Your eyes changed glory shines over me now freedom fills my heart, I'm free in your glory to look up and see the glory of the Lord. Look up and be changed. From Glory to Glory.

Possess Me, Holy Spirit

Exodus 33: 9-11 And it came to pass, as Moses entered into the tabernacle, the cloudy pillar descended, and stood at the door of the tabernacle, and the Lord talked with Moses. And all the people saw the cloudy pillar stand at the tabernacle door: and all the people rose up and worshipped, every man in his tent door. And the Lord spake unto Moses face to face, as a man speaketh unto his friend. And he turned again into the camp: but his servant Joshua, the son of Nun, a young man, departed not out of the tabernacle.

Years ago, there was a woman named Katherine Kuhlman. She was known as one who loved the Holy Spirit. Repeatedly, in her meetings, she would tell the people how much she loved the Holy Spirit

The Holy Spirit was more real to her than any human on this earth.

The Spirit of God descended and the Azusa Street Revival in 1906. There is a house where they have Katherine Kuhlman's pulpit. And I thought back in the Bible, how many times the anointing of God would be transferred, even through pieces of clothing and articles. And I thought, God if your anointing could be an apron or a handkerchief, why not in this pulpit

Every day when I wake up, my prayer is to possess me, Holy Spirit. Take every part of me possess every part of me. Even as Joshua, Moses, his servant, did not depart from the tabernacle, did not depart from the presence. I don't want to depart from your presence Holy Spirit.

Never take your presence from me, I want us well in Your presence all the days of my life.

I want to dwell in that inner sanctuary. I love you Holy Spirit. He will my best friend. You are the one that I live for. The air that I breathe. Be the presence of Your glory. And I pray today, take all of me Holy Spirit.

Possess every fiber of my being, weighed on you, Lord. Holy Spirit. You are my helper. You lead me you guide me into all truth.

Holy Spirit, Your presence is more real to me than the presence of any person on this earth. I yield my spirit to you now. Possess every fiber of my being, possess every molecule in my body

I soak in your presence today. Holy Spirit, draw close to me, fill me with Your Glory. I wait. I wait on your presence. I wait in your glory. Father God, I lay aside every weight of this world. Father God, I lay aside every hindrance and every distraction that would hinder me from your presence. Behold, I said the Promise of My Father upon you, but tarry in the city of Jerusalem. Until you are an endued with power from on high.

But you shall receive power when the Holy Spirit has come upon you. And you shall be witnesses to Me, in Jerusalem, and all Judea and Samaria, and to the end of the earth.

Jesus, you told us to wait. You told us to Terry until we are endued with power from on high. Lord, You said that we would receive power when the Holy Spirit has come upon us. We would be your witnesses. So, Father God, I come, and I wait on you. Father God, I press through into your presence. I wait until your power comes. For you said that if I would tarry and if I would wait upon you that your power would come upon my life.

Father God, I know that everything that I would ever do for you would flow out of the place of intimacy with Your Holy Spirit, fruitfulness and power in life and ministry flow out of the secret place of the Most High God

so, I wait, and I wait upon you now. So, possess me and so fill me with your Spirit that your power would be upon me

why wait - why wait Till.

Holy desperation

Psalm 63:1, 2 O God, thou art my God; early will I seek thee: my soul thirsteth for thee, my flesh longeth for thee in a dry and thirsty land, where no water is; To see thy power and thy glory, so as I have seen thee in the sanctuary.

So, I have looked for you in the sanctuary to see your power and your Glory.

Psalm 42: 1, 2 As the deer pants for the water brooks, so pants my soul for you, oh God. My soul thirsts for God for the living God When shall I come and appear before God? Father God, I come before Your presence today. God my soul is thirsty for you Father my flesh is longing for the very manifested presence of God. I'm hungry and I am desperate for you Lord I can't live without Your presence. You promise that if I search for You and if I seek You with all my heart that I will find You. I'm searching, I'm longing, draw close to me Holy Spirit. I'm desperate for the reality of your glory in my life.

Father God, you say if anyone thirsts, let him come and drink of the river of life.

I thirst father as the deer would go to the living waters and drink, so Father God, I come to the living waters of Your presence, and I drink the living waters of Your spirit.

You fill me with the living waters to satisfy this hunger in my spirit Father God, there is one thing that I desire there is one thing that I long for to see Your Power and Your Glory. I thirst, fill me God.

The Holy Place

2 Chronicles 5: 7 And the priests brought in the ark of the covenant of the Lord unto his place, to the oracle of the house, into the most holy place, even under the wings of the cherubims:

2 Chronicles 5: 11 And it came to pass, when the priests were come out of the holy place: (for all the priests that were present were sanctified, and did not then wait by course:

2 Chronicles 5: 13, 14 It came even to pass, as the trumpeters and singers were as one, to make one sound to be heard in praising and thanking the Lord; and when they lifted up their voice with the trumpets and cymbals and instruments of musick, and praised the Lord, saying, For he is good; for his mercy endureth for ever: that then the house was filled with a cloud, even the house of the Lord; So that the priests could not stand to minister by reason of the cloud: for the glory of the Lord had filled the house of God.

Father, let your glory fill your house once again. Father as we join in with the hosts of heaven, in that heavenly worship, let your glory come and fill the house of God. Lord, we receive your glory right now. Father God, we lift a heavenly sound of worship to you. And as our worship ascends, may Your glory descend upon us now. Fill the house of God with the cloud of glory. Your glory fills the house even as Moses cried, to see your glory, So Father God, I cry, show me Your glory. Show me Your glory.

Jesus, I thank you, that you made the way for us to come into the Holy of Holies where the Ark of your presence dwells. We make our way from the outer courts, into the holy place through the blood of the sacrifice of Your Son Jesus, we make our way and we come into the fullness of where Your glory dwells. Father God, I see Your light, your radiance it shines upon me. I am overcome and I have done in your presence Your glory overwhelms me. Your glory surrounds me in the Holy of Holies My house is filled with Your glory my temple is filled with Your glory open my eyes I see the radiance of the countenance of Your glory. I lay down in your glory even as the priests could not continue to stand because of the weight of Your glory. I cannot stand in Your glory. I lay down in Your glory. Your glory fills me. Your glory saturates. I see Your goodness passing by. I see Your glory all around me. I want to know You. I want to walk with You. Show me now Your way Father God. Let Your presence go before me Your presence, Your presence covers us Your glory surrounds us.

Solitude With God

Solitude with God and Your child will be called the Prophet of the highest.

For You will go before the face of the Lord, to prepare his ways so the child grew and became strong in spirit, and was in the deserts, till the day of His manifestation to Israel.

Now in the morning, having risen a long while before daylight, He went out and departed to a solitary place. And there He prayed.

However, the report went around concerning Him more and great multitudes came together to hear and to be healed by Him of their infirmities.

So, He often withdrew into the wilderness and prayed.

Father God, even as You <u>drew</u> John the Baptist, into the wilderness, for years, You prepared him in a wilderness place. So, Father God, we come into the wilderness today we withdraw from the things of this world. To come away and be with You.

Matthew 6:6 But thou, when thou prayest, enter into thy closet, and when thou hast shut thy door, pray to thy Father which is in secret; and thy Father which seeth in secret shall reward thee openly.

Father God, I come into the secret place. I come into the secret chamber of prayer and hidden devotion. Father God, I withdraw from the things of this world from the voices around me. Lord, I withdraw into the place of solitude. Jesus even as you would go to a solitary place and there You would pray even as You would often withdraw into the wilderness, to be alone with God. So, Father God, I withdraw into the wilderness. There I seek Your face. I seek Your face and Your voice for when I pray in secret You will reward openly. Father, I lay aside the things of this earth so that I could just be with you. For Jesus would say nothing, except what He heard his father saying. And He would do nothing except what He saw his father doing.

So, I withdraw into the wilderness. I withdraw into the wilderness into the place of prayer. Father God, just You and me I look to see Your face. I love to hear Your voice speak for Your servant is listening I wait upon Your Presence Father in this place you take from me the burdens and the weights of this world. Let my vision be consumed with one thing Your face or voice? Speak Your servant is listening

Holy Ground

So, I have come down to deliver them out of the hand of the Egyptians, and to bring them up from that land to a good and large land, to a land flowing with milk and honey.

Malachi 3: 2, 3 But who may abide the day of his coming? and who shall stand when he appeareth? for he is like a refiner's fire, and like fullers' soap: And he shall sit as a refiner and purifier of silver: and he shall purify the sons of Levi, and purge them as gold and silver, that they may offer unto the Lord an offering in righteousness.

Father God as I approach Your presence, Father God, as I draw nearer to the living presence, for the Holy God, Lord, I take the shoes off my feet. For this is all the rounds for Your presence is here. Lord, wherever your presence is His Holy Father, I bow before you. Lord, I bow before the awesomeness of a holy God. Lord, this is holy ground. Where your presence is, is holy Lord, I am in awe in Your presence. Father God, even as Isaiah saw the Lord high and lifted, and he saw the seraphim over the throne and as Isaiah saw You, he was done in your presence and the seraphim. He took the living coals of fire and touched his lips his sin was purged. So, Father God, I pray to take the living coals of Your fire and touch my lips today.

Touch My legs. Make me holy as You are holy. Let me know Your holiness even as I stand on the holy ground let me know Your holiness.

Father God may Your Holiness permeate me. Let Your Holiness permeate every fiber of my being you are holy God, You are holy and I worship You. I worship You in the beauty of Your holiness. I lift holy hands to Your presence, and I bow my face to the ground I prostrate myself before You in the presence of Your holiness. Your host holding the whole earth is full of Your glory spirit of burning consuming now the Spirit of God is holy, holy, holy. Cover me with the blood of Jesus that I would be holy. I am purged from my sin Your fire touches me now. I can feel Your fire going through my being purging my sin, hearing my cry. Father, HOLY, HOLY, HOLY.

The Revival Mantle

2 Kings 2: 9-14 And it came to pass, when they were gone over, that Elijah said unto Elisha, Ask what I shall do for thee, before I be taken away from thee. And Elisha said, I pray thee, let a double portion of thy spirit be upon me. And he said, Thou hast asked a hard thing: nevertheless, if thou see me when I am taken from thee, it shall be so unto thee; but if not, it shall not be so. And it came to pass, as they still went on, and talked, that, behold, there appeared a chariot of fire, and horses of fire, and parted them both asunder; and Elijah went up by a whirlwind into heaven. And Elisha saw it, and he cried, My father, my father, the chariot of Israel, and the horsemen thereof. And he saw him no more: and he took hold of his own clothes, and rent them in two pieces. He took up also the mantle of Elijah that fell from him, and went back, and stood by the bank of Jordan; And he took the mantle of Elijah that fell from him, and smote the waters, and said, Where is the Lord God of Elijah? and when he also had smitten the waters, they parted hither and thither: and Elisha went over.

God had poured out in Whales 100 years ago. I realized that God was once again extending an invitation to this generation, to pick up the mantle of revival to lay hold of those mantles of power once again and anointing that God had poured out in past generations. And I knew that God was saying it's available to you. All you have to do is pick it up. Father God, I thank You that now was the time to lay hold the most mantles of revival. Father God, You're giving this generation a holy invitation to once again, pick up and carry the mantle of awakening and power Lord, I'm not looking for a mantle that another man carried. Father God, I'm looking for the mantle that Jesus wore. Father God, I'm not asking for a double portion of the anointing that was on a man. But I'm asking for a double portion of the Spirit that rested on the Son of God. The unlimited anointing and power of the Holy Spirit. Father God, would You pour it out again upon the church, Father poured out now, across our nation. Let men and women rise in this hour and let them be girded with the mantle, that Jesus wore a mantle of power and glory the mantle of humility, and make this release the double portion of your glory Father God, make service of the Most High God.

Also by Bill Vincent

Building a Prototype Church: Divine Strategies Released
Experience God's Love: By Revival Waves of Glory School of the Supernatural
Glory: Expanding God's Presence
Glory: Increasing God's Presence
Glory: Kingdom Presence of God
Glory: Pursuing God's Presence
Glory: Revival Presence of God
Rapture Revelations: Jesus Is Coming
The Prototype Church: Heaven's Strategies for Today's Church
The Secret Place of God's Power
Transitioning Into a Prototype Church: New Church Arising
Spiritual Warfare Made Simple
Aligning With God's Promises
A Closer Relationship With God
Armed for Battle: Spiritual Warfare Battle Commands
Breakthrough of Spiritual Strongholds
Desperate for God's Presence: Understanding Supernatural Atmospheres
Destroying the Jezebel Spirit: How to Overcome the Spirit Before It Destroys You!
Discerning Your Call of God

Glory: Expanding God's Presence: Discover How to Manifest God's Glory

Glory: Kingdom Presence Of God: Secrets to Becoming Ambassadors of Christ

Satan's Open Doors: Access Denied

Spiritual Warfare: The Complete Collection

The War for Spiritual Battles: Identify Satan's Strategies

Understanding Heaven's Court System: Explosive Life Changing Secrets

A Godly Shaking: Don't Create Waves

Faith: A Connection of God's Power

Global Warning: Prophetic Details Revealed

Overcoming Obstacles

Spiritual Leadership: Kingdom Foundation Principles

Glory: Revival Presence of God: Discover How to Release Revival Glory

Increasing Your Prophetic Gift: Developing a Pure Prophetic Flow

Millions of Churches: Why Is the World Going to Hell?

The Supernatural Realm: Discover Heaven's Secrets

The Unsearchable Riches of Christ: Chosen to be Sons of God

Deep Hunger: God Will Change Your Appetite Toward Him

Defeating the Demonic Realm

Glory: Increasing God's Presence: Discover New Waves of God's Glory

Growing In the Prophetic: Developing a Prophetic Voice

Healing After Divorce: Grace, Mercy and Remarriage

Love is Waiting

Awakening of Miracles: Personal Testimonies of God's Healing Power

Deception and Consequences Revealed: You Shall Know the Truth and the Truth Shall Set You Free

Overcoming the Power of Lust

Are You a Follower of Christ: Discover True Salvation

Cover Up and Save Yourself: Revealing Sexy is Not Sexy

Heaven's Court System: Bringing Justice for All

The Angry Fighter's Story: Harness the Fire Within

The Wrestler: The Pursuit of a Dream

Beginning the Courts of Heaven: Understanding the Basics

Breaking Curses: Legal Rights in the Courts of Heaven

Writing and Publishing a Book: Secrets of a Christian Author

How to Write a Book: Step by Step Guide

The Anointing: Fresh Oil of God's Presence

Spiritual Leadership: Kingdom Foundation Principles Second Edition

The Courts of Heaven: How to Present Your Case

The Jezebel Spirit: Tactics of Jezebel's Control

Heaven's Angels: The Nature and Ranking of Angels

Don't Know What to Do?: Discover Promotion in the Wilderness

Word of the Lord: Prophetic Word for 2020

The Coronavirus Prophecy

Increase Your Anointing: Discover the Supernatural

Apostolic Breakthrough: Birthing God's Purposes

The Healing Power of God: Releasing the Power of the Holy Spirit

The Secret Place of God's Power: Revelations of God's Word

The Rapture: Details of the Second Coming of Christ

Increase of Revelation and Restoration: Reveal, Recover & Restore

Restoration of the Soul: The Presence of God Changes Everything

Building a Prototype Church: The Church is in a Season of Profound of Change

Keys to Receiving Your Miracle: Miracles Happen Today

The Resurrection Power of God: Great Exploits of God

Transitioning to the Prototype Church: The Church is in a Season of Profound of Transition

Waves of Revival: Expect the Unexpected

The Stronghold of Jezebel: A True Story of a Man's Journey

Glory: Pursuing God's Presence: Revealing Secrets

Like a Mighty Rushing Wind

Steps to Revival

Supernatural Power

The Goodness of God

The Secret to Spiritual Strength

The Glorious Church's Birth: Understanding God's Plan For Our Lives

God's Presence Has a Profound Impact On Us

Spiritual Battles of the Mind: When All Hell Breaks Loose, Heaven Sends Help

A Godly Shaking Coming to the Church: Churches are Being Rerouted

Relationship with God in a New Way

The Spirit of God's Anointing: Using the Holy Spirit's Power in You

The Magnificent Church: God's Power Is Being Manifested

Miracles Are Awakened: Today is a Day of Miracles

Prepared to Fight: The Battle of Deliverance

The Journey of a Faithful: Adhering to the teachings of Jesus Christ

Ascension to the Top of Spiritual Mountains: Putting an End to Pain Cycles

After Divorce Recovery: When I Think of Grace, I Think of Mercy and Remarriage

A Greater Sense of God's Presence: Learn How to Make God's Glory Visible

Do Not Allow the Enemy to Steal: To a Crown of Righteousness, a Crown of Thorns

There Are Countless Churches: What is the Cause of Global Doom?

Creating a Model Church: The Church is Undergoing Considerable Upheaval

Developing Your Prophetic Ability: Creating a Flow of Pure Prophetic Intent

Christ's Limitless Riches Are Unsearchable: God Has Chosen Us to Be His Sons

Faith is a Link Between God's Might and Ours

Increasing the Presence of God: The Revival of the End-Times Is Approaching

Getting a Prophecy for Yourself: Unlocking Your Prophecies with Prophetic Keys

Getting Rid of the Jezebel Spirit: Before the Spirit Destroys You, Here's How to Overcome It!

Getting to Know Heaven's Court System: Secrets That Will Change Your Life

God's Resurrected Presence: Revival Glory is Being Released

God's Presence In His Kingdom: Secrets to Becoming Christ's Ambassadors

God's Healing Ability: The Holy Spirit's Power is Being Released

God's Power of Resurrection: God's Great Exploits

Heaven's Supreme Court: Providing Equal Justice for All
Increasing God's Presence in Our Lives: God's Glory Has Reached New Heights
Jezebel's Stronghold: This is the Story of an Actual Man's Journey
Making the Shift to the Model Church: The Church Is In the Midst of a Major Shift
Overcoming Lust's Influence: The Way to Victory
Pursuing God's Presence: Disclosing Information
The Plan to Take Over America: Restoring, We the People and the Power of God
Revelation and Restoration Are Increasing: The Process That Reveals, Recovers, and Restores
Burn In the Presence of the Lord
Revival Tidal Waves: Be Prepared for the Unexpected
Taking down the Demonic Realm: Curses and Revelations of Demonic Spirits
The Apocalypse: Details about Christ's Second Coming
The Hidden Resource of God's Power
The Open Doors of Satan: Access is Restricted
The Secrets to Getting Your Miracle
The Truth About Deception and Its Consequences
The Universal World: Discover the Mysteries of Heaven
Warning to the World: Details of Prophecies Have Been Revealed
Wonders and Significance: God's Glory in New Waves
Word of the Lord
Why Is There No Lasting Revival: It's Time For the Next Move of God
A Double New Beginning: A Prophetic Word, the Best Is Yet to Come

Your Most Productive Season Ever: The Anointing to Get Things Done

Break Free From Prison: No More Bondage for the Saints

Breaking Strongholds: Taking Steps to Freedom

Carrying the Glory of God: Igniting the End Time Revival

Breakthrough Over the Enemies Attack on Resources: An Angel Called Breakthrough

Days of Breakthrough: Your Time is Now

Empowered For the Unprecedented: Extraordinary Days Ahead

The Ultimate Guide to Self-Publishing: How to Write, Publish, and Promote Your Book for Free

The Art of Writing: A Comprehensive Guide to Crafting Your Masterpiece

The Non-Fiction Writer's Guide: Mastering Engaging Narratives

Spiritual Leadership (Large Print Edition): Kingdom Foundation Principles

Desperate for God's Presence (Large Print Edition): Understanding Supernatural Atmospheres

From Writer to Marketer: How to Successfully Promote Your Self-Published Book

Unleashing Your Inner Author: A Step-by-Step Guide to Crafting Your Own Bestseller

Becoming a YouTube Sensation: A Guide to Success

Watch for more at https://revivalwavesofgloryministries.com/.

About the Author

Bill Vincent is no stranger to understanding the power of God. Not only has he spent over twenty years as a Minister with a strong prophetic anointing, he is now also an Apostle and Author with Revival Waves of Glory Ministries in Litchfield, IL. Along with his wife, Tabitha, he, leads a team providing apostolic oversight in all aspects of ministry, including service, personal ministry and Godly character.

Bill offers a wide range of writings and teachings from deliverance, to experiencing presence of God and developing Apostolic cutting edge Church structure. Drawing on the power of the Holy Spirit through years of experience in Revival, Spiritual Sensitivity, and deliverance ministry, Bill now focuses mainly on pursuing the Presence of God and breaking the power of the devil off of people's lives.

His books 50 and counting has since helped many people to overcome the spirits and curses of Satan. For more information or to keep up with Bill's latest releases, please visit www.revivalwavesofgloryministries.com. To contact Bill, feel free to follow him on twitter @revivalwaves.

Read more at https://revivalwavesofgloryministries.com/.

About the Publisher

Accepting manuscripts in the most categories. We love to help people get their words available to the world.

Revival Waves of Glory focus is to provide more options to be published. We do traditional paperbacks, hardcovers, audio books and ebooks all over the world. A traditional royalty-based publisher that offers self-publishing options, Revival Waves provides a very author friendly and transparent publishing process, with President Bill Vincent involved in the full process of your book. Send us your manuscript and we will contact you as soon as possible.

Contact: Bill Vincent at rwgpublishing@yahoo.com

CPSIA information can be obtained
at www.ICGtesting.com
Printed in the USA
BVHW072315200423
662720BV00013B/1191